Happy 3

To a

very dear

Dena

with love

Grace

June 7th 1991

Biblical passages are from the King James
Version of the Holy Bible unless specified as
NIV (New International Version) or RSV
(Revised Standard Version).

*This book is dedicated to all those
touched by the spirit of the living God.*

Table of Contents

Women of the Bible

And Adam called his wife's name Eve;
because she was the mother of all living.
Genesis 3:20

And it shall come to pass that your sons
and daughters shall prophesy.
Joel 2:28

*The Biblical story of God's creation of Eve
as a woman of independent thought fore-
shadows God's words to Joel: that the words
of women will be of equal value to those of
men in the future greatness of Israel.*

*In the following passages, women of the
Old Testament emerge as matriarchs,
psalmists, petitioners, lovers, prophetesses,
judges, and queens. These women speak in
disbelief, joy, and bereavement, and in loyalty to their families, people, and God. Their
voices exert a strong influence on Hebrew
history.*

So Sarah laughed to herself, saying, After I
have grown old, and my husband is old,
shall I have pleasure? . . . Shall I indeed
bear a child, now that I am old?
*Sarah, wife of Abraham and mother of
Isaac, Genesis 18:12, 13 (RSV)*

Sing ye to the Lord, for he hath triumphed
gloriously; the horse and his rider hath he
thrown into the sea.
*Miriam, sister of Moses, Exodus 15:21
[Exodus of the Jews from Egypt]*

Why should the name of our father be done
away from among his family, because he
hath no son? Give unto us therefore a pos-
session among the brethren of our father.
*Mahlah, Noah, Hoglah, Milcah and
Tirzah, Numbers 27:4
[Early petition in favor of women's rights]*

My lord, I am the woman that stood by
thee here, praying unto the Lord. For this
child I prayed; and the Lord hath given me
my petition which I asked of him: Therefore also I have lent him to the Lord; as
long as he liveth he shall be lent to the
Lord.
*Hannah, mother of Samuel, judge of Israel,
I Samuel 1:26-28*

Intreat me not to leave thee, or to return
from following after thee: for whither thou
goest, I will go; and where thou lodgest, I
will lodge: thy people shall be my people,
and thy God my God: Where thou diest,
will I die, and there will I be buried.
Ruth, Ruth 1:16-17
*[Speaking to Naomi, her mother-in-law,
thus committing herself to the people of
Israel and their God.]*

Praise ye the Lord for the avenging of
Israel, when the people willingly offered
themselves. Hear, O ye kings; give ear, O
ye princes; I, even I, will sing unto the
Lord; I will sing praise to the Lord God of
Israel.
*Deborah, prophetess and judge of Israel,
Judges 5: 2-3*
*[After delivering Israel from Sisera, an ene-
my captain]*

For how can I endure to see the evil that
shall come unto my people? or how can I
endure to see the destruction of my kindred?
*Esther, Queen to King Ahasuerus, Esther
4:16, 8:5-6*
*[Admitting her Judaism to her husband, the
king, and thereby averting the evil plot to
have the Jews destroyed.]*

7

The New Testament Gospel stories of Jesus illustrate both the love and compassion which he showed women, and the trust and faith which he elicited from women around him. His mother, the faithful Virgin Mary, and Mary Magdalene, who, when "healed of evil spirits," became a loyal follower of Jesus, represent the saint and sinner or "whole woman" ministered to by him. Jesus meets women not in the temple, but teaches in the home of Martha and her sister, prophesies to a non-Jewish woman at a well, and heals women who believe in him.

Paul, a missionary to the Gentiles, conforms to tradition in advising against women speaking in churches, yet refers warmly to Priscilla and other Christian women as co-workers in the faith. Envisioning the new order, Paul writes, "There is neither Jew nor Greek, . . . bond nor free, . . . male nor female, for ye are all one in Christ Jesus." Galatians 3:28

Jesus taught that each person is special in the eyes of God. Women of faith and spirit speak of their belief that all people share equally in the goodness of God.

Blessed are thou among women, and blessed is the fruit of thy womb.
Elisabeth, mother of John the Baptist,
Luke 1:42
[*Speaking to Mary, mother of Jesus*]

My soul doth magnify the Lord, And my spirit hath rejoiced in God my Saviour. For he hath regarded the low estate of his handmaiden: for, behold, from henceforth all generations shall call me blessed. For he that is mighty hath done to me great things; and holy is his name. And his mercy is on them that fear him from generation to generation. He hath shewed strength with his arm; he hath scattered the proud in the imagination of their hearts. He hath put down the mighty from their seats, and exalted them of low degree. He hath filled the hungry with good things; and the rich he hath sent empty away. He hath holpen his servant Israel, in remembrance of his mercy; As he spake to our fathers, to Abraham, and to his seed for ever.
Mary, mother of Jesus, Luke 1:46-55
[*The Magnificat*]

Martha: Lord, dost thou not care that my sister hath left me to serve alone? bid her therefore that she help me.

Jesus: Martha, Martha, thou art careful and troubled about many things: But one thing is needful: and Mary hath chosen that good part, which shall not be taken away from her.

Luke 10:40-42

[*Referring to Mary's desire to listen to his teachings*]

Woman at the well: Sir, I perceive that thou art a prophet. . . . I know that Messias cometh, which is called Christ: when he is come, he will tell us all things.

Jesus: I that speak unto thee am He.

Woman (to her people): Come, see a man, which told me all things that ever I did: is not this the Christ?

Woman of Samaria, John 4:19, 25, 26, 29

Woman, chronically ill: If I may touch but his clothes, I shall be whole.

Jesus: Who touched my clothes? . . . (*Seeing woman*) Daughter, thy faith hath made thee whole; go in peace, and be whole of thy plague.

Mark 5:28, 30, 34

Woman of Canaan: Lord, Son of David, have mercy on me! My daughter is suffering terribly from demon-possession. . . . Lord, help me!
Jesus: Woman, you have great faith! Your request is granted.
Matthew 15:22, 25, 28 (NIV)

Angels at the sepulchre: Woman, why weepest thou?
Mary Magdalene: Because they have taken away my Lord, and I know not where they have laid him.
Jesus (unrecognized): Woman, why weepest thou? Whom seekest thou?
Mary Magdalene: Sir, if thou have borne him hence, tell me where thou hast laid him, and I will take him away.
Jesus: Mary.
Mary Magdalene: Rabboni [Master]. *As she recognizes Jesus, risen from the tomb.*
John 20: 13, 15, 16

Women of the Middle Ages, Renaissance, Reformation, and Beyond

Early Christian women and their families often suffered persecution for their faith. After Rome fell, monasteries offered many women education and spiritual nurture. Other women influenced their families and communities through the strength of their faith. Women mystics spoke from within and without the convent, some revered as visionaries, even saints, and some tortured as witches. The burning of witches, begun in Europe in the 3rd Century, continued there and in America through the 17th Century. During the Renaissance and Reformation, women increasingly questioned established church doctrines, and, moved by the spirit, believed, as did the Quakers, that women as well as men must speak according to their "inner lights."

I am a Christian; no wickedness is carried on by us!
Blandina, 2d C. slave girl martyred by Rome

I entreat the omnipotent Lord my God that in this instance you neither inflict injury on anyone nor suffer it yourselves: wherefore lay aside your diabolical emblems of warfare.
Brigit of Kildare, 6th C. Patron Saint of Ireland

But sometimes I behold within this light another light which I name "the Living Light itself" . . . And when I look upon it every sadness and pain vanishes from my memory, so that I am again as a simple maid and not as an old woman.
Hildegard of Bingen, 12th C. German mystic

The Lord, in fact has placed us as an example, as models and mirrors . . . for our sisters whom he has called to the same vocation, so that in turn they may be mirrors and models for those living in the world.
St. Clare, 12th C. disciple of St. Francis of Assisi

How strait is the way that leads to life!
And how narrow is the gate through which
one must enter! Thus there are few who
walk along this path and who pass through
this gate. And if there are some who walk
along the path for a moment, O how rare
are those who know how to persevere
there!
St. Clare

And don't spend the time not allocated to
prayer chattering. Let nothing draw you
away from prayer—or anything else—except
necessity, obedience or charity, as I have
said.
*Catherine of Siena, 14th C. Italian mystic
and advisor to popes.*

. . . rejoicing to be our Father, rejoicing too
to be our Mother; and rejoicing yet again to
be our true Husband, with our soul his be-
loved wife. And Christ rejoices to be our
Brother and our Savior too.
Julian of Norwich, 14th C. English recluse

In God's name! let us go on bravely!
*Joan of Arc, 15th C. mystic, martyred as a
witch*

Joan: I hear voices telling me what to do. They come from God.
de Beaudricourt: They come from your imagination.
Joan: Of course. That is how the messages of God come to us.
George Bernard Shaw, St. Joan

Madame, if I, at this very moment, held my son, and all the kingdoms of the world together, in my grasp, I would hurl them to the bottom of the sea, rather than peril the salvation of my soul.
Jeanne D'Albret, 15th C. Queen of Navarre

When I took the habit, the Lord at once showed me how great are His favours to those who use force with themselves in His service. No one realized that I had gone through all this; they all thought I had acted out of sheer desire. At the time my entrance into this new life gave me a joy so great that it has never failed me even to this day, and God converted the aridity of my soul into the deepest tenderness. Everything connected with the religious life caused me delight.
St. Teresa of Avila. 16th C. Spanish mystic

While still a child I heard that God spoke through those who preach. This made a deep impression on me and gave me a strong urge to listen to them, even though I was so young that I understood very little of what they said except the narrative parts, which I recounted on my return home.
Venerable Marie of the Incarnation, 17th C. Canadian mystic

Now let us see if any of you, blind Priests, can speak after this manner, and see if it be not a better Sermon than any of you can make, who are against Women's Speaking.
Margaret Fell, 17th C. English Quaker

It was never in my heart to slight any man, but only that man should be kept in his place and not sit in the room of God.
Anne Hutchinson, exile from Massachusetts Bay Colony, 17th C.

In obedience to the will of the Lord I came, and in His will I abide faithful to the death.
Mary Dyer, 17th C. Quaker martyr, hanged in Boston

God gives talent for sacred use and it is so unjust that not only women (considered inept) but also men (who, simply by being thus, consider themselves wise) are forbidden the interpretation of the Holy Scriptures if they are not erudite and virtuous.
Sor Juana Inés de la Cruz, 17th C. Mexican, first woman theologian in the Americas

It came into my mind that though I am not a man nor a minister of the Gospel, and so cannot be employed in such a worthy employment as they were, yet if my heart were sincerely devoted to God, and if I were inspired with a true zeal for his glory and did really desire the salvation of souls, I might do something more than I do.
Susanna Wesley, mother of John Wesley, 18th C.

It is not I that speak, it is Christ who dwells in me. I converse with Christ; I feel him present with me, as sensibly as I feel my hands together.
Ann Lee, 18th C. founder of Shakers in America

How can we live an interior life until some of our natural rubbish is removed?
St. Elizabeth Seton, founder, Sisters of Charity, early 19th C.

When so rich a harvest is before us, why do we not gather it? All is in our hands if we will but use it.
St. Elizabeth Seton

Through piety and gratitude we come to the deepest recess of peace and true contentment.
St. Elizabeth Seton

Women of the 19th Century

Women showed great courage when they began to speak in public about issues of faith and of justice, especially for slaves and women. They encountered stinging criticism which questioned their loyalty to their family, church, and country.

The church in many places is a sort of potter's field, where the gifts of woman, as so many strangers, are buried.
Phoebe Palmer, Holiness Revivalist

I live—no, not I, but the Heart of Christ lives in me.
St. Madeleine Sophie, founder of Order of Sacred Heart for women

All I ask of our brethren is that they take their feet off our necks, and permit us to stand upright on the ground which God has designated us to occupy.
Sarah Grimké, abolitionist and suffragette

[I am] firm in the blessed, the eternal doctrines preached by Jesus and by every child of God from the creation of the world, especially . . . the doctrine which Jesus most emphatically taught, that the kingdom of God is within man.
Lucretia Coffin Mott, Quaker minister and suffragette

Children, I speak to God and God speaks to me.
Sojourner Truth, abolitionist, born a slave
[Beginning her public speeches]

There are too many men and women; there is too little Humanity . . . There is a dearth of understanding, of nakedness of spirit. All of us are over-dressed.
Anna Kingsford, theosophist

'Oh, God, give me a name with a handle to it. Oh, that I had a name with a handle!' And it came to me, and that same moment, like a voice as true as God is true: 'Sojourner TRUTH.' And my heart leaped for joy—Sojourner Truth. 'Why,' said I, 'thank you, God. That is a good name. Thou art

my last master and thy name is Truth, so shall Truth be my abiding name until I die.'
Sojourner Truth

Where did your Christ come from? . . . From God and a woman. Man had nothing to do with him. If the first woman God ever made was strong enough to turn the world upside down all alone, these women together ought to be able to turn it back and get it right-side up again. And now that they are asking to do it, the men better let 'em.
Sojourner Truth

To be really great in little things, to be truly noble and heroic in the insipid details of every-day life, is a virtue so rare as to be worthy of canonization.
Harriet Beecher Stowe, writer

. . . and now . . . we are called on to set the example of a new state of society,—noble, simple, pure, and religious; and women can do more towards this even than men, for women are the real architects of society.
Harriet Beecher Stowe

Just as a mother would not love a child the better for its being turned into a model of perfection . . . but does love it the more deeply every time it tries to be good, so I do hope and believe our great Father does not wait for us to be good and wise to love us, but loves us, and loves to help us in the very thick of our struggle.
Juliana Horatia Ewing

I never spoke with God,
Nor visited in heaven;
Yet certain am I of the spot
As if the chart were given.
Emily Dickinson, poet

. . . How much bondage and suffering a woman escapes when she takes the liberty of being her own physician of both body and soul.
Elizabeth Cady Stanton, social reformer

The religious persecution of the ages has been done under what was claimed to be the command of God. I distrust those people who know so well what God wants them to do to their fellows, because it always coincides with their own desires.
Elizabeth Cady Stanton

What if I am a woman? Did [God] not raise up Deborah to be mother, and a judge in Israel? Did not Queen Esther save the lives of the Jews? And Mary Magdalene first declare the resurrection of Christ from the dead? . . . Saint Paul declared that it was a shame for a woman to speak in public, yet our great High Priest and Advocate did not condemn the woman for a more notorious offence than this. . . . Did Saint Paul but know of our wrongs and deprivations, I presume he would make no objections to our pleading in public for our rights.
Maria Stewart, feminist

I'm not denyin' the women are foolish: God Almighty made 'em to match the men.
George Eliot, pen name of Mary Ann Evans, writer

When I found I had crossed dat *line*, I looked at my hands to see if I was de same pusson. There was such a glory ober ebery ting; de sun came like gold through the trees, and ober the fields, and I felt like I was in Heaben.
Harriet Tubman, abolitionist, born a slave

Woman's great mission is to train imma-
ture, weak, and ignorant creatures, to obey
the laws of God; . . . first in the family,
then in the school, then in the neighbor-
hood, then in the nation, then in the
world—that great family of God whom the
Master came to teach and to save.
Catharine Beecher, writer

. . . and I shall earnestly and persistently
continue to urge all women to the practical
recognition of the old Revolutionary max-
im, "Resistance to tyranny is obedience to
God."
Susan B. Anthony, suffragette

If a law commands me to *sin I will break
it*; if it calls me to *suffer*, I will let it take
its course *unresistingly*. The doctrine of
blind obedience and unqualified submission
to *any human* power, whether civil or eccle-
siastical, is the doctrine of despotism, and
ought to have no place among Republicans
and Christians.
Angelina Grimké Weld

There is every encouragement for you to labor and pray ... because the abolition of slavery ... has been the theme of prophecy. ... Are not the Christian negroes of the south lifting their hands in prayer for deliverance, just as the Israelites did when their redemption was drawing nigh?
Angelina Grimké Weld, abolitionist

I know not what you believe of God, but I believe He gave yearnings and longings to be filled, and that He did not mean all our time should be devoted to feeding and clothing the body.
Lucy Stone, suffragette

There was also growing within me an almost passionate devotion to the ideals of democracy, and when in all history had these ideals been so thrillingly expressed as when the faith of the fisherman and the slave had been boldly opposed to the accepted moral belief that the well-being of a privileged few might justly be built upon the ignorance and sacrifice of the many?
Jane Addams, social reformer

Hearts are not touched without Religion. Religion was not given us from above in impressions and generalities, but in habits of thought and action, in love of God and of mankind, carried into action.
Florence Nightingale, English nurse

Love is not something put upon a shelf, to be taken down on rare occasions with sugar-tongs and laid on a rose-leaf.
Mary Baker Eddy, founder of Christian Science

Fatherhood and motherhood exist in the complete human being. . . . The Life-giving quality of Mind is Spirit, not matter. The ideal man corresponds to creation, to Intelligence, and Truth. The ideal woman corresponds to Life and Love. We have not as much authority, in Divine Science, for considering God masculine, as we have for considering Him feminine, for Love imparts the highest idea of Deity.
Mary Baker Eddy

No one can claim to be called Christian
who gives money for the building of war-
ships and arsenals.
Belva Lockwood, lawyer

We have found sickness and poverty to re-
lieve, widows to protect, advice to be given
in every possible difficulty or emergency,
teachers and Bible women to be trained, . . .
We have found use for every faculty, natural and acquired, that we possessed, and
have coveted all that we lacked.
*Isabella Thoburn, late 19th C. missionary
wife*

There were angry men confronting me and
I caught the flashing of defiant eyes, but
above me and within me, there was a spirit
stronger than them all. At that moment not
the combined powers of earth and hell
could have tempted me to do otherwise than
stand firm. . . . "Do you think," says a
voice in my ear, "that Christ would have
done so?" "I think he would . . . "
*Antoinette Brown Blackwell, first ordained
woman in the United States*

The especial genius of women, I believe to be electrical in movement, intuitive in function, spiritual in tendency.
Margaret Fuller, feminist

What a wonderful thing is Life! Life everlasting, going on continuously, in steps, the ever-coming new ones taking the place of the old worn-out ones—how beautiful!
Charlotte Perkins Gilman, social critic

Notwithstanding the poverty of my outside experience, I have always had a significance for myself, and every chance to stumble along my straight and narrow little path, and to worship at the feet of my Deity, and what more can a human soul ask for?
Alice James, diarist

People need joy. Quite as much as clothing. Some of them need it far more.
Margaret Collier Graham, writer

Women of the Early Twentieth Century

The militancy of the abolitionists and suf-fragettes who believed that the principles of their faith meant justice and equality for all was replaced in the early 20th Century by a concern for individual fulfillment through a life of faith and devotion to Christian teachings.

Faith is the first factor in a life devoted to service. Without faith, nothing is possible. With it, nothing is impossible.
Mary McLeod Bethune, educator

Next to God, we are indebted to women, first for life itself, and then for making it worth having.
Mary McLeod Bethune

I would rather walk with God in the dark than go alone in the light.
Mary Gardiner Brainard, poet

This is the wonderful thing about the pure in heart—they do see God.
Corra May Harris, writer

All that is necessary to make this world a better place to live is to love—to love as Christ loved, as Buddha loved.
Isadora Duncan, dancer

Religion is love; in no case is it logic.
Beatrice Potter Webb, English reformer

Jesus loves me, this I know
For the Bible tells me so.
Anna Bartlett Warner, writer

Now I'm a believer, and I try to live a Christian life, but I'd as soon hear a surveyor's book read out, figgers an' all, as try to get any simple truth out o' most sermons.
Sarah Orne Jewett, writer

I would, therefore, always urge every seeker after the deep things of God to ignore emotions and care only for convictions.
Hannah Whitall Smith, Quaker temperance leader

It is only the women whose eyes have been washed clear with tears who get the broad vision that makes them little sisters to all the world.
Dorothy Dix, journalist

This is the "new" religion; yet it is older than the universe. It is God's own thought put into practical form. . . . a religion which says: "I am all goodness, love, truth, mercy, health. I am a necessary part of God's universe. I am a divine soul, and only good can come through me or to me.
Ella Wheeler Wilcox, poet and journalist

The miracles of the church seem to me to rest not so much upon faces or voices or healing power coming suddenly near to us from afar off, but upon our perceptions being made finer, so that for a moment our eyes can see and our ears can hear what is there about us always.
Willa Cather, writer

Loving, like prayer, is a power as well as a process. It's curative. It is creative.
Zona Gale, writer

Intuition is a spiritual faculty and does not explain, but simply points the way.
Florence Scovel Shinn

I have elsewhere tried to show that Art is not the handmaid of Religion, but that Art in some sense springs out of Religion, and that between them is a connecting link, a bridge, and that bridge is Ritual.
Jane Harrison, English archeologist

The power of Christianity, the power of all religion, is sustained by that strange capacity we call faith, a word very commonly used and very commonly misunderstood.
Edith Hamilton, scholar

I am in the [Salvation] Army because I believe it is the greatest movement in the world for lifting men and women out of their sorrows and sin, and seeing how it is doing this in greater numbers every day, love it better every day.
Evangeline Booth, first woman general in the Salvation Army

When Africans speak of the personality of God, they speak like the Arabian Nights or the last chapters of the Book of Job; it is ... the infinite power of imagination with which they are impressed.
Isak Dinesen, pen name of Karen Blixen, Danish writer

Christian [white] women would reach out for the same hand as [I, a black woman, did ... but] I know that the dear Lord will not receive it if you [whites] are crushing me beneath your feet.
Charlotte Hawkins Brown, black feminist orator

We are all making a crown for Jesus out of these daily lives of ours, either a crown of golden, divine love, studded with gems of sacrifice and adoration, or a thorny crown, filled with the cruel briars of unbelief, or selfishness, and sin, and placing it upon His brow.
Aimée Semple McPherson, founder, Four Square Gospel Church

The beauty of the Old Testament does not exceed that of a Negro prayer.
Zora Neale Hurston, writer

Sometimes God gits familiar wid us women-folks too and talks His inside business. He told me how surprised He was 'bout y'all [men] turning out so smart after Him makin' yuh different; and how surprised y'all is goin' tuh be if you ever find out you don't know half as much 'bout us as you think you do. It's so easy to make yo'self out God Almighty when you ain't got nothin' tuh strain against but women and chickens.
Zora Neale Hurston

For me the meaning of life is centered in our Redemption by Christ and . . . what I see in the world I see in its relation to that. I don't think that this is a position that can be taken half-way or one that is particularly easy in these times to make transparent in fiction.
Flannery O'Connor, writer

Love is not getting, but giving. It is sacrifice. And sacrifice is glorious!
Joanna Field, English psychologist

Christ likes us to prefer truth to him because, before being Christ, he is truth.
Simone Weil, French theologian

To believe in something not yet proved and to underwrite it with our lives; it is the only way we can leave the future open.
Lillian Smith, writer

"For God so loved the world, that He gave His only begotten Son, that whosoever believeth in Him should not perish, but have everlasting life." With these words the scales fell from my eyes and the light came flooding in. My sense of inferiority, my fear of handicaps, dropped away. "Whosoever," it said. No Jew nor Gentile, no Catholic nor Protestant, no black nor white; just "whosoever." It meant that I, a humble Negro girl, had just as much chance as anybody in the sight and love of God.
Mary McLeod Bethune

Women of the Modern Day

*Women in the last fifty years have been
affected by world events: the Depression,
World War II and the Holocaust, nuclear
power, feminism, and the challenges to authority in civil and human rights. Many
women of faith have found a place and a
greater voice in their churches and syn-
agogues. Women's theology, and liberation
theologies in general, uphold personal spiritual experience, emphasize speaking of God
in new ways, and affirm the liberating power of the Spirit for all who are oppressed.*

I feel like a pencil in God's hand. . . . God
writes through us, and however imperfect
instruments we may be, he writes beautiful-
ly. . . . He deigns to work through us. Is
that not marvellous?
Mother Teresa, missionary nun to India

I found god in myself and I loved her
fiercely.
Ntozake Shange, playwright

I told them: "Holiness is not a luxury—you are all invited to it." I said this to Hindus, Moslems, Jains, Parsees, Christians.
Mother Teresa

I didn't know what she was saying when she moved her lips in a Baptist church or a Catholic cathedral or, less often, in a synagogue, but it was obvious that God could be found anywhere. . . .
Lillian Hellman, writer

Blues are the songs of despair, but gospel songs are the songs of hope.
Mahalia Jackson, singer

Perhaps in His wisdom the Almighty is trying to show us that a leader may chart the way, may point out the road to lasting peace, but that many leaders and many peoples must do the building.
Eleanor Roosevelt, humanitarian

Do not wait for leaders; do it alone, person to person.
Mother Teresa

Prepared by the Inventor of life, the Bible
is our instruction and service manual. It is
the guidebook on how to live in an unfair
world. And it comes with the guarantee
that those who follow it will have success
in life.
Marabel Morgan, writer

Sometimes I've known the Spirit within
as a nudge, as direction, or reminder, or
conscience.
Catherine Marshall, writer

The gospel nearly explodes with the star-
tling mystery that God forgives. . . . [but
the] actual difficulty involved in putting the
teachings of Jesus (on the subject of for-
giveness) into practice, lies halfway between
how simple it looks in the New Testament
and how impossible it appears when we've
been deeply hurt by someone.
Doris Donnelly, theologian

A religious awakening which does not
awaken the sleeper to love has roused him
in vain.
Jessamyn West, writer

Some of the pathfinders found that membership in a church or temple was not as meaningful for them as literature, music, or climbing a mountain to seek that silence unadorned by illusion, where the presence of God may be felt.
Gail Sheehy, writer

The Christian church has always had a place for the righteous agnostics, the unconscious believers, those great humanitarians who have worked in labor unions, grape fields, native hospitals, and black ghettoes to fight oppression; . . . The company of uncanonized saints surely stretches far into the ranks of the "unbelievers." But does it include those for whom the personal religious question is the primary one—How can I give *my* life meaning, dignity, purpose?
Sallie TeSelle, theologian

The spiritual quest begins, for most people, as a search for meaning. . . . A mystical experience, however brief, is validating for those attracted to the spiritual search. The mind now knows what the heart had only hoped for.
Marilyn Ferguson, journalist

Prayer does not use any artificial energy, it doesn't burn up any fossil fuel, it doesn't pollute. Neither does song, neither does love, neither does the dance.
Margaret Mead, anthropologist

Even those whose lives had appeared to be ticking imperturbably under their smiling clock-faces were often trying, like me, to evolve another rhythm with more creative pauses in it. . . .

When we start at the center of ourselves, we discover something worthwhile extending toward the periphery of the circle. We find again some of the joy in the now, some of the peace in the here, some of the love in me and thee which go to make up the kingdom of heaven on earth.
Anne Morrow Lindbergh, writer

And this I do believe above all . . . that I must believe in my fellow men—that I must believe in myself—that I must believe in God—if life is to have any meaning.
Margaret Chase Smith, U. S. Senator

We literally heard one another down to a word that was *our* word, and that word was ourselves. . . . No one can take this journey of women but the women themselves who are involved. To put it on "Jesus," or the priest, or the therapist is to perpetuate the same dependency we are now seeking to throw off.
Nelle Morton, theologian and feminist

From uncovering my hoard of personal riches, I extrapolate the secret hoards in all women . . . Our yeasty richness will leaven and change the world.
Sonia Johnson, exiled Mormon

In some not altogether frivolous sense God needs to be liberated from our theology. Theology is not a tabernacle to contain the One who is Ahead, but it is a sign on the way, and thus is provisional. Thus the theologian is not only protester and prophet, if she is lucky, but also pilgrim.
Joan Arnold Romero, theologian

Why indeed must "God" be a noun? Why not a verb—the most active and dynamic of all? . . . And isn't the Verb infinitely more personal than a mere static noun?
Mary Daly, feminist theologian

"Godding" [is an] activity learned from the life and teachings of Jesus: making good / making justice / making love / making God incarnate in this world.
Isabel Carter Heyward, Episcopal priest

The image of "Christ the Liberator" is part of the ideology of liberation theology and is intended to express the notion that salvation in Christ includes political and social as well as individual spiritual salvation.
Pauli Murray

In early Christian times women were treated with relative honor when they submitted themselves to the yoke of the Church; they bore witness as martyrs side by side with men. But they could take only a secondary place as participants in worship; the "deaconesses" were authorized to carry out only such lay tasks as caring for the sick and aiding the poor.
Simone de Beauvoir, writer

If I love with my Spirit, I don't have to think so hard with my head.
Peggy Cahn

Christian women can see in Jesus a unique revelation of true personhood: One who helped both men and women to understand their own total personhood.
Letty M. Russell, theologian

The creation of man first and of woman last constitutes a ring composition whereby the two creatures are parallel. . . . She is not an afterthought; she is the culmination. . . .
Phyllis Trible, theologian

We cannot . . . become caterpillars again. The raising of women's consciousness has raised our own and we cannot deny what we know. We can and must be ministers of reconciliation.
Sister Juliana Casey, Catholic nun

It is imperative that women be permeated by a spirit that is truly dialogic. We need to be women who are open, who will listen, who experience an inner freedom. We must be confident, unafraid, critical yet compassionate, gentle yet strong.
Sister Theresa Kane, Catholic nun

If you are good and have something to say, the church cannot keep you down . . . . Build a level of spiritual resiliency. Take yourself seriously, but develop a sense of humor.
Valerie Russell, religious administrator

To be a Jew in the twentieth century is to be offered a gift. If you refuse, wishing to be invisible, you choose death of the spirit. . . .
Muriel Rukeyser, poet

There is no act, no sermon, no parable in the whole Gospel that borrows its pungency from female perversity; nobody could guess from the words and deeds of Jesus that there was anything "funny" about woman's nature.
Dorothy L. Sayers, writer

The herstorian recognizes and affirms the noble impulse, the thrust of promise and fulfillment which lies behind the biblical epic . . . but looks before, behind, beyond, and even outside the tradition as well as at it for her affirmation. . . .
Sheila Collins, writer

One of the things Jesus did was to step aside from the organized religion of his time because it had become corrupt and bogged down with rules. Rules became more important than feeding the hungry.
Corita Kent, graphic artist

A commitment to love and justice demands the transformation of social structures as well as of hearts.
Mary E. Hunt, educator

. . . The position of woman today might have been foretold at the beginning, when, instead of creating her out of dust, the Lord waited until he could build her out of a strong, healthy, germ-proof bone.
Hannah Greenbaum Solomon, founder of National Council of Jewish Women

The feminine—as woman, as anima and as the body—is like Noah's Ark and the nativity stable: it receives and actively holds within itself whatever is poured in . . . it carries these embryos until they are transformed into something new and then releases them into life.
Sue Harris, writer

Fountainhead, source, spring of all goodness, living wind: That is also language for
God, in which human beings have expressed their relationship to God without
resorting to sexist or familial language.
Dorothee Sölle, theologian

The witch that smolders within every woman who cared and dared enough to become
a theologian or philosopher in the first
place seems to be crying out these days:
"Light my fire!" The qualitative leap of
those flames of spiritual imagination and
cerebral fantasy can be a new dawn.
Mary Daly

I do not abandon the Mother God. I need
her. But I hold onto God the Father, too.
The mythical throne I look to is shared, a
source of inspiration for shared parenting.
Diane Tennis, writer

Now what if you introduce to . . . a man
the idea that the God we really pray to is
not the "masculine" Old Testament God,
but the power-through-gentleness-and-love
Jesus-type God who . . . has as his role the
role of mother, as we understand it in
earthly terms.
Sonia Johnson

God is wherever there is real desire, real longing, for connection . . . God *is* in the connections.
Beverly Harrison, theologian

Surely God means nature to sensitise us to other silences and rhythms. . . . All nature is a sign of the sacred in our midst.
Meinrad Craighead, artist

God knows (*she* knows) that women try.
Gloria Steinem, feminist

Between the process of creating and the sense of calling, womanist theology will one day present itself in full array, reflecting the divine spirit that connects us all.
Delores S. Williams, theologian

What is it about the Word of God that makes it so important for the proclaimer of that Word to be of a certain sex, and that sex male?
Nelle Morton, theologian and feminist

Christian and Jewish women (and many who consider themselves neither) have discovered a common ancestor in Lilith who, according to Jewish myth, was Adam's first wife and claimed equal status with him but flew away when she discovered that equality was not in the cards for her.
Sheila Collins, writer

My belief in the perfect God does not allow me to think that the Lord would favor one sex over the other in any area of life.
Blu Greenberg, Jewish feminist

Female God language is especially important in the Jewish context because so much of the Jewish religious enterprise involves talking, not about God, but *to* God. . . . We do not yet know the potential and gift that comes with the entrance of Jewish women into Judaism. We do not fully know the lineaments of God-She. But we do know that She is inevitable and insuppressible.
Rita Gross, educator

Religion controls inner space; inner space controls outer space.
Zsuzsanna E. Budapest, writer

Feminist spirituality proclaims wholeness, healing love, and spiritual power not as hierarchical, as *power over*, but as *power for*, as enabling power. It proclaims *the Goddess* as the source of this power, as the enabling context of human lives and of a nonhierarchical, nonauthoritarian, noncompetitive community.
Elizabeth Schüsler Fiorenza, Biblical scholar

As a classicist I became acquainted with the cult of the Goddess 25 years ago and remain tolerably fond of the Great Mother.
Rosemary R. Ruether, Catholic theologian

The long sleep of Mother Goddess is ended. May She awaken in each of our hearts— Merry meet, merry part, and blessed be.
Starhawk, pen name of Miriam Simos, feminist

I remember Jonah accusing God of overlenience, of foolishness, mercy, and compassion. We desperately need the foolishness of God.
Madeleine L'Engle, writer

If my hands are fully occupied in holding on to something, I can neither give nor receive.
Dorothee Sölle

The Jewish heart has always starved unless it was fed through the Jewish intellect.
Henrietta Szold, founder of Hadassah

We [blacks] were in church Sunday morning to Saturday night. It was our whole life, our social life, our religious training, everything. My mother didn't believe in movies, so I didn't go to the movies. . . . But I enjoyed the church services. I sang in the choir and played the piano and the organ. . . . It was that kind of thing that saved us. Church became a shelter for us.
Cicely Tyson, actress

If Rosa Parks had not sat down, Martin King would not have stood up.
Unknown

Somehow I hope in this resurrection experience the will will be created within the hearts, and minds, and the souls, and the spirits of those who have the power to make these changes come about.
Coretta Scott King, civil rights leader

Now I was empowered to minister the sacrament of One in whom there is no north or south, no black or white, no male or female—only the spirit of love and reconciliation drawing us all toward the goal of human wholeness.
Pauli Murray, lawyer and Episcopal priest

I may yet be driven stark raving mad by the church's slowness to respond and change. And yet, many of us do awaken to conversion, and find our lives remolded, energized, and transported to new places of mind and heart.
Linda Kusse-Wolfe, Quaker minister

Well, it's a good thing to trust in Providence. But I believe the Almighty likes a little cooperation now and again.
Frances Parkinson Keyes, writer

The Christian life is a life embedded in dailiness, not one in which the uncertainties of the future overshadow the tasks of the present. . . . What keeps the Christian going, cheek to jowl with the stuff of everyday existence, is the knowledge of God written on his or her heart.
Linda Clark, educator, sacred music

I have listened to the realm of the Spirit. I have heard my own soul's voice, and I have remembered that love is the complete and unifying thread of existence.
Mary Casey, Catholic theologian

"Liberty and justice for all" must include women. Nothing less will do.
Annette Daum, Jewish religious educator

We are an immeasurable speck in the immense galaxies. Yet we are part of a divine creativity. . . . To sense the awesome presence of God in this world is to gain insight into who we are, where we belong, to find our place in the scheme of things.
Sharon Blessum Sawatzky, educator

Dear God. Dear stars, dear trees, dear sky, dear peoples. Dear Everything. Dear God.
Alice Walker, writer

Love doesn't just sit there like a stone, it has to be made, like brick; re-made all the time, made new.
Ursula K. LeGuin, writer

The Bible and Christian tradition give us a different understanding of reality . . . The sacred and the secular are not two different sectors of life, or two different areas in space or time; they are two different ways of seeing and responding to the whole of reality. . . . It means that any ground is holy, because God is everywhere—not only in places officially designated for worship but in homes, streets, offices, factories.

. . . This technological culture, now spreading round the world, is the first in human history to deny the very presence of the sacred within itself as it attempts to dominate the earth's limited resources.
Sally Cunneen, educator

This is perhaps the greatest lesson we learned from our patients: *LIVE so you do not have to look back and say: "God, how I have wasted my life."*
Elisabeth Kubler-Ross, medical author

What can we commit our lives to that will help us become more authentic as persons? That is the religious issue for all, whether or not we are terminal.
Elisabeth Kubler-Ross

How much did I hear of religion as a child? Very little, and yet my heart leaped when I heard the name of God. I do believe every soul has a tendency toward God.
Dorothy Day, Catholic social reformer

The only answer in this life, to the loneliness we are all bound to feel, is community. The living together, working together, sharing together, loving God and loving our brother, and living close to him in community so we can show our love for Him.
Dorothy Day

People who have a religion should be glad, for not everyone has the gift of believing in heavenly things. . . . a religion, it doesn't matter which, keeps a person on the right path. It isn't the fear of God but the upholding of one's own honor and conscience.
Anne Frank, Holocaust victim

The secret of seeing is to sail on solar wind. Hone and spread your spirit, till you yourself are a sail, whetted, translucent, broadside to the merest puff.
Annie Dillard, writer

God is Wind—Breath—Spirit. . . . Fresh winds of the Spirit bring God's power and gentleness into the sanctuary where we can only bow in awe, and then dare to hear and heed God's latest call to us.
Lavon Bayler, Christian liturgist

Yes, I have doubted. I have wandered off the path. I have been lost. But I always returned. It is beyond the logic I seek. It is intuitive—an intrinsic, built-in sense of direction. I seem always to find my way home. My faith has wavered but has saved me.
Helen Hayes, actress

We don't know light until we know darkness.
Louisa Kennedy, wife of Iran hostage

When everyone is aligned with the knowledge that *each* is part of God, the consciousness of civilization will reflect peace—peace within. Recognize that within each individual is the divine cosmic truth that you term God.
Shirley MacLaine, actress

. . . the unexplainable, the ultimately un-knowable. . . . we call that something "spirit"—the spirit of this people—which has no limitations and is indestructible. This spiritual strength is eternal. It is transmitted from generation to generation, almost unwittingly.
Golda Meir, former Prime Minister of Israel

We cannot always understand the ways of Almighty God—the crosses which He sends us, the sacrifices which He demands of us. . . . But we accept with faith and resignation His holy will with no looking back to what might have been, and we are at peace.
Rose Fitzgerald Kennedy, matriarch

Strange, is it not, that among all the wonders man has worked, and the discoveries he has made, there is only one field to which he has paid no attention; it is that of the miracle that God has worked from the first: the miracle of children.
Maria Montessori, educator

How are we to find time for the inner life
when the outer demands on our mercy are
so unending and urgent? The answer can
only be in rigorous pruning, in lopping off
much that is superfluous, in "ordering" our
lives, first things first.
Mildred Binns Young, Quaker

Now to me, nothing can ever be religion
unless it takes eternity into account, and
makes all life continuous, binding the living
with those others, making for the perfection (completion) of each one of us in time
to come, binding generation to generation
on earth, too, by means of an unbroken tradition, a religious system.
Alice Seligsberg, Zionist

In spite of everything I still believe that
people are really good at heart. I simply
can't build up my hopes on a foundation
consisting of confusion, misery, and
death. . . . yet, if I look up into the heav-
ens, I think that it will all come right, that
this cruelty too will end, and that peace
and tranquillity will return again.
Anne Frank